TASTE OF GREECE

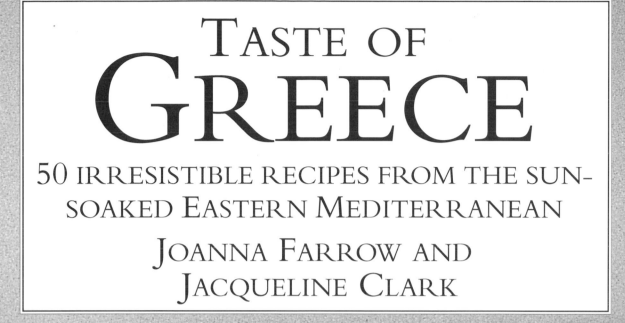

Taste of
GREECE

50 IRRESISTIBLE RECIPES FROM THE SUN-SOAKED EASTERN MEDITERRANEAN

JOANNA FARROW AND
JACQUELINE CLARK

SMITHMARK

This edition published in 1997 by
SMITHMARK Publishers Inc.
a division of US Media Holdings Inc.
16 East 32nd Street
New York
New York 10016

SMITHMARK books are available for bulk purchase for sales and promotion
and premium use. For details, write or call the manager of special sales,
SMITHMARK Publishers Inc.
16 East 32nd Street
New York, New York 10016
(212) 532-6600

Produced by Anness Publishing Limited
Hermes House
88-89 Blackfriars Road
London SE1 8HA

ISBN 0-7651-9555-0

Publisher: Joanna Lorenz
Senior Cookery Editor: Linda Fraser
Designers: Nigel Partridge and Ian Sandom
Photography and styling: Michelle Garrett, assisted by Dulce Riberio
Food for photography: Jacqueline Clark and Joanna Farrow
Illustrator: Anna Koska

Printed and bound in Singapore by Star Standard Industries Pte. Ltd.

1 3 5 7 9 10 8 6 4 2

CONTENTS

INTRODUCTION

The countries of the eastern Mediterranean - Greece, Turkey, Cyprus, Egypt - and the Middle East share a cuisine based on the influence of the sea, the climate and the history of the area. It is a fascinating mix of simply-cooked foods based on wonderful fresh ingredients whose flavors are drawn out by the hot sun, rice and ground meat dishes designed to make a substantial meal out of inexpensive or scarce ingredients, and recipes incorporating exotic spices and flavorings.

In ancient times the area surrounding the Mediterranean Sea was colonized by the Phoenicians, Greeks and Romans, who cultivated wheat, olives and grapes. These, in turn, became bread, oil and wine, three components that are still very important in today's Mediterranean diet. With the building of ships came import and export, with the result that spices and flavorings were introduced through North Africa and Arabia. Saffron, cloves, chilies, ginger and allspice are still popular all over the Mediterranean, appearing in both sweet and savory dishes.

A market stall in southern Turkey with an abundance of tomatoes, onions, potatoes and grapes.

This exotic influence, together with the fact that our impressions of the Eastern Mediterranean are largely formed by visits there during the summer, makes it difficult to imagine that the agriculture of the region does suffer from bad weather. However, drought on the land and storms at sea do ruin crops and the fisherman's catch. Because of this, the most basic foods are, even today, a celebration of life to the Greek people. Bread is an important staple and always accompanies a meal, be it a bowl of soup or a platter of grilled fish.

A Greek street market is a fascinating scene, full of color and bustle. Greek vegetables have an inviting irregularity about them: uneven colorings, knobby skins and nonsymmetrical shapes are a sure indication that the flesh inside will be full of flavor, far superior to the mass-produced, artificially grown produce of colder climates. The dishes cooked using them are a joy to eat, and even the simplest tossed salad of tomatoes and leaves, sprinkled with olive oil and seasoning, is worthy of serving solo.

In the Eastern Mediterranean, local and specialized variations of a mezze (a spread of appetizers) are popular with both locals and visitors, and, in Greece, can be accompanied by either ouzo or wine. Sheep's and goat's

yogurt are hung to produce thickened cheeses that are bottled in spiced olive oil; these are delicious spread on warm toast. Dressed tomatoes, fried halloumi or keflotyri cheese drizzled with lemon juice and pepper, and a bowl of garlic-flavored Greek yogurt are often served as a lavish first course.

The Mediterranean Sea is tiny in relation to the world's larger seas and oceans. It is also relatively shallow, warm, low in natural food supplies and more polluted. Despite all these factors, the Mediterranean has hundreds of different species of fish and crustacea. A visit to a Greek taverna illustrates how freshly caught fish, cooked simply, can be unbeatable. Perfectly fresh fish, grilled with a basting of olive oil, garlic and herbs, needs little more embellishment, except perhaps a crisp salad and light wine. On a more elaborate scale, fish stews and soups are typical all around the Mediterranean.

Unlike the vegetable and fish dishes, however, meat recipes are less abundant. The countryside

The day's catch is brought home to Crete packed in salt.

Shopping for vegetables and local news in a Turkish market.

around the Mediterranean can be quite harsh, with no lush, green fields for animals to graze. Lamb and goat are favorite meats. The meat of the young kid is particularly popular in parts of Greece, in Corsica and the Middle East. The Greek Orthodox Church formerly had strict rules concerning "lean" days, when meat was forbidden, so many special feast dishes using meat were created to celebrate the end of these regular fasts.

The countries surrounding the Mediterranean produce a seemingly inexhaustible quantity and variety of grains and pulses. Wheat, the most ancient cereal grown in the region, predominates. Wheat flour is also used to make the highly popular filo pastries of Greece, Turkey, Lebanon and North Africa. It is skillfully shaped and stretched to form a transparent sheet that is then brushed with olive oil or melted butter and folded into layers. When cooked, it resembles a very light and crisp puff pastry. Filo is used in many sweet and savory classics such as the Middle Eastern

chicken and apricot pie.

Desserts produced in Greece and elsewhere in the Mediterranean take full advantage of the glorious abundance of fresh fruits. For a special occasion, a selection of seasonal fruits such as figs, plums, apricots, peaches, melons and cherries makes a stunning finale. These can be arranged on a platter lined with grape or fig leaves, some fruits cut open decoratively, and the whole platter scattered with crushed ice. Honey is plentiful and therefore much favored as a sweetener, often teamed with nuts and dates. The most popular nuts are almonds, pistachios and pine nuts, which are native to the region.

Fresh salads, simply prepared main courses, spiced grains, delicious breads and fruit flavored with nuts and honey – these are the tastes of Greece and the Eastern Mediterranean to be enjoyed to their fullest through the recipes in this delicious collection.

INGREDIENTS

CHEESE

The Greek cheeses most widely available outside Greece are feta and halloumi. Feta is made from goats milk and is a popular ingredient in salads. Halloumi is generally made from ewe's milk and is often fried, then served with lemon juice and pepper.

CHICK-PEAS

This pulse looks like a pale golden hazelnut and is sold either dried or ready cooked. Chick-peas have a nutty

flavor and are widely used in stews from North Africa to Spain. In Greece and Turkey they are puréed with olive oil to produce hummus, a delicious dip. Soak them for up to 4 hours, depending on how old they are, in order to tenderize them.

CUMIN SEEDS

These dark, spindly seeds are often married with coriander when making the spicy dishes that are typical of the Eastern Mediterranean. They are also ground to make tahini.

DATES

Although fresh dates are quite widely available, imported from Egypt, Israel and California, the dried variety remains invaluable. Fresh dates should be plump and slightly wrinkled. They have a rich, honeylike flavor and dense texture.

EGGPLANT

Although eggplant originated from Asia, it is featured in dishes from Greece and every Mediterranean country. There are many different varieties,

including green, white and yellow, but the plump purple variety is the most common. Look for firm, taut, shiny-skinned specimens with green stalks. Eggplant is sometimes salted and drained before cooking, which helps to extract bitter juices and makes them absorb less oil during cooking.

FENNEL

This white bulb of overlapping leaves and green, feathery fronds has a fresh aniseed flavor and can be eaten cooked or raw. Its flavor complements fish and chicken very well. Choose firm, rounded bulbs, and use the fronds for garnishing.

FIGS

This fruit is associated with Greece and all the Mediterranean countries. Different varieties vary in color, from dark purple to green to a golden yellow, but all are made up of hundreds of tiny seeds, surrounded by soft pink flesh that is perfectly edible. Choose firm unblemished figs, which just yield to the touch.

FRESH HERBS

Huge bundles of fresh coriander are a familiar sight in Eastern Mediterranean markets, their warm, pungent aroma rising at the merest touch. The leaves impart a distinctive flavor to soups, stews, sauces and spicy dishes when

added toward the end of cooking. They are also used sparingly in salads and yogurt dishes. Mint also features in many recipes as an integral part and as a garnish, its fresh taste adding zest to creamy dishes and pulses. Parsley, dill, oregano, basil and many other fresh herbs all play an important part.

GARLIC

Sold in "strings" or as separate bulbs, the main consideration when buying garlic is that the cloves are plump and firm. Used crushed, sliced or even whole, garlic develops a smooth, gentle flavor with long, slow cooking. Used raw in salads, mayonnaise and sauce, garlic has a hot, fierce impact.

HARISSA

A fiery hot paste made from a blend of chilies, garlic, cumin, coriander and cayenne. It can be bought in small jars.

MUSSELS

Mussels usually need to be scrubbed and have the beard – the hairy tuft attached to the shell – removed. Any open mussels should be discarded before cooking if they do not close after a sharp tap. Mussels vary in size, and the shell can be blue-black to dappled brown. They are easy to cook – just steam for a few minutes in a covered pan.

OLIVE OIL

Together with its healthy qualities, olive oil is indispensable to Greek

cooking for its fine, nutty flavor. The richest oil comes from the first cold pressing of the olives, producing a golden green "virgin" oil.

OLIVES

The fruit of one of the earliest known trees native to the Mediterranean. There are hundreds of varieties, differing widely in size, quality and taste. Color depends purely on ripeness – the fruit changes from yellow to green, violet, purple, brown and finally black when fully ripened. Fresh olives are picked at the desired stage of ripeness, then soaked in water, bruised and immersed in brine to produce the familiar-tasting result. They can be bought whole or pitted, sometimes stuffed with peppers, anchovies or nuts, or bottled with flavorings such as garlic, coriander, chili and herbs.

PEPPERS

In Greece, Turkey and the Middle East bell peppers are served stuffed, filled with couscous, rice, herbs, spices, dried fruits, nuts, cheese and sometimes meat. Another way of making the most of the flavor of bell peppers is to grill them until the skins are charred, rub off and discard the skins, then marinate the peppers in olive oil.

PINE NUTS

These little nuts are used in both sweet and savory dishes. They are often served with marinated vegetables, and are an important ingredient in sweet pastries.

SEA BASS

This is quite an expensive fish and is usually sold and cooked whole. The flesh is soft and delicate and needs careful attention when cooking. Methods include poaching, steaming, grilling and baking.

SHRIMP

These vary enormously in size: the classic Mediterranean shrimp is large, about 8 inches. When prawns are cooked over a fierce heat, such as a barbecue, the shell is often left on to protect the flesh from charring.

SQUID

Squid vary in size, from the tiny specimens that can be eaten whole, to the larger varieties, which are good for stuffing, grilling or stewing. The flesh is sweet and tender when either cooked briefly over a fierce heat or given a long cooking over a low heat.

TAHINI

A smooth oily paste ground from sesame seeds and used to give a nutty flavor to Middle Eastern dishes.

TUNA

A large oily fish belonging to the same family as mackerel. The flesh, which is sold in steaks or large pieces, is dark red and very dense, and has a tendency to dry out when cooked. Marinating before cooking helps keep the flesh moist, as does basting frequently while cooking. Tuna can be baked, fried, grilled or stewed.

YOGURT

This live dairy product (pasteurized milk combined with two beneficial bacteria) is a typical ingredient in the cuisines of the Eastern Mediterranean and is used to make soft cheese. Greek yogurt, made from either ewe's or cow's milk, is thick and creamy.

SOUPS AND APPETIZERS

Soups can be light and refreshing like
Avgolemono or substantial enough, when eaten
with bread, to make a nourishing meal, such as
Green Lentil Soup. Cold soups are a feature of
the cuisine of the Eastern Mediterranean — they
are yogurt-based, usually mixed with cucumber
and garlic, and spiked with mint. Appetizers are
also a specialty of this area and are made from all
types of food, both cooked and uncooked. Called
"mezze" or "mezedes," they form an important
part of the meal. The selection in this chapter
presents recipes for cheese, seafood and vegetables
as a taster in itself.

SPICED MUSSEL SOUP

Chunky and colorful, this Turkish fish soup is like a chowder in its consistency. It's flavored with harissa sauce, more familiar in North African cooking.

3–3½ pounds fresh mussels
⅔ cup white wine
3 tomatoes
2 tablespoons olive oil
1 onion, finely chopped
2 garlic cloves, crushed
2 celery stalks, thinly sliced
bunch of scallions, thinly sliced
1 potato, diced
1½ teaspoons harissa sauce
3 tablespoons chopped fresh parsley
ground black pepper
thick yogurt, to serve (optional)

SERVES 6

1 Scrub the mussels, discarding any damaged ones or any open ones that do not close when tapped with a knife.

2 Bring the wine to a boil in a large saucepan. Add the mussels and cover with a lid. Cook for 4–5 minutes until the mussels have opened wide. Discard any mussels that remain closed. Drain the mussels, reserving the cooking liquid. Reserve a few mussels in their shells for garnish and shell the rest.

3 Peel the tomatoes and dice them. Heat the oil in a pan and fry the onion, garlic, celery and scallions for 5 minutes.

4 Add the shelled mussels, reserved liquid, potato, harissa sauce and tomatoes. Bring just to a boil, reduce the heat and cover. Simmer gently for 25 minutes, or until the potatoes are breaking up.

5 Stir in the parsley and pepper and add the reserved mussels. Heat through for 1 minute. Serve hot with a spoonful of yogurt, if you like.

GREEN LENTIL SOUP

Lentil soup is an Eastern Mediterranean classic, varying in its spiciness according to region. Red or puy lentils make an equally good substitute for the green lentils used here.

1 cup green lentils
5 tablespoons olive oil
3 onions, finely chopped
2 garlic cloves, thinly sliced
2 teaspoons cumin seeds, crushed
¼ teaspoon ground turmeric
2½ cups chicken or vegetable stock
salt and ground black pepper
2 tablespoons coarsely chopped
fresh cilantro, to finish

SERVES 4–6

1 Put the lentils in a saucepan and cover with cold water. Bring to a boil and boil rapidly for 10 minutes. Drain.

2 Heat 2 tablespoons of the oil in a pan and fry two of the onions with the garlic, cumin and turmeric for 3 minutes, stirring. Add the lentils, stock and 2½ cups water. Bring to a boil, reduce the heat, cover and simmer gently for 30 minutes, until the lentils are soft.

3 Fry the third onion in the remaining oil until golden.

4 Use a potato masher to lightly mash the lentils and make the soup pulpy. Reheat gently and season with salt and pepper to taste. Pour the soup into bowls. Stir the chopped fresh cilantro into the fried onion and scatter on the soup. Serve with warm bread.

SPICY PUMPKIN SOUP

Pumpkin is popular all over the Mediterranean and it's an important ingredient in Middle Eastern cooking, from which this soup is inspired. Ginger and cumin give the soup its spicy flavor.

2 pounds pumpkin, peeled and
seeds removed
2 tablespoons olive oil
2 leeks, trimmed and sliced
1 garlic clove, crushed
1 teaspoon ground ginger
1 teaspoon ground cumin
3¾ cups chicken stock
salt and ground black pepper
cilantro leaves, to garnish
4 tablespoons plain yogurt, to serve

SERVES 4

1 Cut the pumpkin into chunks. Heat the oil in a large pan and add the leeks and garlic. Cook gently until softened.

2 Add the ginger and cumin and cook, stirring, for another minute. Add the pumpkin and the chicken stock and season with salt and pepper. Bring to a boil and simmer for 30 minutes, until the pumpkin is tender. Process the soup, in batches if necessary, in a blender or food processor.

3 Reheat the soup and serve in warmed individual bowls, with a swirl of yogurt and a garnish of cilantro leaves.

MIDDLE EASTERN YOGURT AND CUCUMBER SOUP

Yogurt is used extensively in Middle Eastern cooking, and it is usually made at home. Sometimes it is added at the end of cooking a dish, to prevent it from curdling, but in this cold soup the yogurt is one of the basic ingredients.

1 large cucumber, peeled
1¼ cups light cream
⅔ cup plain yogurt
2 garlic cloves, crushed
2 tablespoons white wine vinegar
1 tablespoon chopped fresh mint
salt and ground black pepper
sprigs of mint, to garnish

SERVES 4

2 Chill for at least 2 hours before serving. Just before serving, stir the soup again. Pour into individual bowls and garnish with mint sprigs.

1 Grate the cucumber coarsely. Place in a bowl with the cream, yogurt, garlic, vinegar and mint. Stir well and season to taste.

AVGOLEMONO

This is the most popular of Greek soups. The name means egg and lemon, the two important ingredients, which produce a light, nourishing soup. Orzo is Greek, rice-shaped pasta, but you can use any small shape.

7½ cups well-flavored chicken stock
½ cup orzo pasta
3 eggs
juice of 1 large lemon
salt and ground black pepper
lemon slices, to garnish

SERVES 4–6

1. Pour the stock into a large pan, and bring to a boil. Add the pasta and cook for 5 minutes.

2. Beat the eggs until frothy, then add the lemon juice and a tablespoon of cold water. Slowly stir in a ladleful of the hot chicken stock, then add one or two more. Return this mixture to the pan, off the heat, and stir well. Season with salt and pepper and serve immediately, garnished with lemon slices. (Do not let the soup boil once the eggs have been added or it will curdle.)

FRESH TOMATO SOUP

Intensely flavored sun-ripened tomatoes need little embellishment in this fresh-tasting soup. If you buy from the supermarket, choose the ripest looking ones and add the amount of sugar and vinegar necessary, depending on their natural sweetness. On a hot day this soup is also delicious chilled.

3–3½ pounds ripe tomatoes
1⅔ cups well-flavored chicken or vegetable stock
3 tablespoons sun-dried tomato paste
2 teaspoons red wine vinegar
2–3 teaspoons sugar
small handful basil leaves
salt and ground black pepper
basil leaves, to garnish
toasted cheese croutons and sour cream, to serve

SERVES 6

1 Plunge the tomatoes into boiling water for 30 seconds, then refresh in cold water. Peel away the skins and quarter the tomatoes. Put them in a large saucepan and pour on the chicken or vegetable stock. Bring just to a boil, reduce the heat, cover and simmer gently for 10 minutes until the tomatoes are soft.

2 Stir in the tomato paste, vinegar, sugar and basil. Season with salt and pepper, then cook gently, stirring, for 2 minutes. Process the soup in a blender or food processor, then return to the pan and reheat gently. Serve in bowls topped with one or two toasted cheese croutons and a spoonful of sour cream, garnished with basil leaves.

YOGURT CHEESE IN OLIVE OIL

Sheep's milk is widely used in cheese making in the Eastern Mediterranean, particularly in Greece where sheep's yogurt is hung in cheesecloth to drain off the whey before patting into balls of soft cheese. Here it's bottled in olive oil with chili and herbs — an appropriate gift for a "foodie" friend.

1¾ pounds sheep's yogurt
½ teaspoon salt
2 teaspoons crushed dried chilies or
chili powder
1 tablespoon chopped fresh rosemary
1 tablespoon chopped fresh thyme
or oregano
1¼ cups olive oil, preferably garlic-
flavored

FILLS TWO 1 POUND JARS

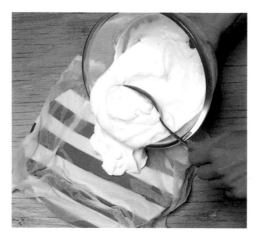

1 Sterilize a 12-inch square of cheesecloth by steeping it in boiling water. Drain and lay over a large plate. Mix the yogurt with the salt and tip on to the center of the cheesecloth. Bring up the sides of the cheesecloth and tie firmly with string.

2 Hang the bag on a kitchen cupboard handle or suitable position where the bag can be suspended with a bowl underneath to catch the whey. Leave for 2–3 days until the yogurt stops dripping.

3 Sterilize two 1-pound glass preserving or jam jars by heating them in the oven at 300°F for 15 minutes.

4 Mix together the chili and herbs. Take teaspoonfuls of the cheese and roll into balls with your hands. Lower into the jars, sprinkling each layer with the herb mixture.

5 Pour the oil on the cheese until completely covered. Store in the fridge for up to 3 weeks.

6 To serve the cheese, spoon out of the jars with a little of the flavored olive oil and spread onto lightly toasted bread.

COOK'S TIP
If your kitchen is particularly warm, find a cooler place to suspend the cheese. Alternatively, drain the cheese in the fridge, suspending the bag from one of the shelves.

SAUTEED MUSSELS WITH GARLIC AND HERBS

These mussels are served without their shells, in a delicious paprika flavored sauce.
Eat them with toothpicks.

2 pounds fresh mussels
1 lemon slice
6 tablespoons olive oil
2 shallots, finely chopped
1 garlic clove, finely chopped
1 tablespoon chopped fresh parsley
½ teaspoon sweet paprika
¼ teaspoon dried chili flakes
parsley sprigs, to garnish

SERVES 4

1 Scrub the mussels, discarding any damaged ones that do not close when tapped with a knife. Put the mussels in a large pan with 1 cup water and the slice of lemon. Bring to a boil for 3–4 minutes and remove the mussels as they open. Discard any that remain closed. Take the mussels out of the shells and drain them on paper towels.

2 Heat the oil in a sauté pan, add the mussels *(left)* and cook, stirring, for a minute. Remove from the pan. Add the shallots and garlic and cook, covered, over a low heat, for about 5 minutes, until soft. Stir in the parsley, paprika and chili, then add the mussels with any juices. Cook briefly. Remove the pan from the heat, cover and let sit for 1–2 minutes to let the flavors mingle. Serve, garnished with parsley.

MARINATED BABY EGGPLANT WITH RAISINS AND PINE NUTS

—

Eggplant is popular in all the Mediterranean countries. Grilled vegetables which are then cooled in an oil and vinegar marinade are a typical starter. Make this recipe a day in advance, to allow the sour and sweet flavors to develop.

12 baby eggplant, halved lengthwise
1 cup extra virgin olive oil
juice of 1 lemon
2 teaspoons red wine vinegar
3 cloves
⅓ cup pine nuts
2 tablespoons raisins
1 tablespoon granulated sugar
1 bay leaf
large pinch of dried chili flakes
salt and ground black pepper

SERVES 4

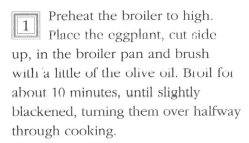

1. Preheat the broiler to high. Place the eggplant, cut side up, in the broiler pan and brush with a little of the olive oil. Broil for about 10 minutes, until slightly blackened, turning them over halfway through cooking.

2. To make the marinade, put the remaining olive oil, the lemon juice, vinegar, cloves, pine nuts, raisins, sugar and bay leaf in a bowl. Add the chili flakes and salt and pepper and mix well.

3. Place the hot eggplant in an earthenware or glass bowl, and pour on the marinade. Allow to cool, turning the eggplant once or twice. Serve cold.

BROILED VEGETABLE TERRINE

A colorful, layered terrine, using all the vegetables associated with the Mediterranean.

2 large red bell peppers, quartered,
cored and seeded
2 large yellow bell peppers, quartered,
cored and seeded
1 large eggplant, sliced lengthwise
2 large zucchini, sliced lengthwise
6 tablespoons olive oil
1 large red onion, thinly sliced
½ cup raisins
1 tablespoon tomato paste
1 tablespoon red wine vinegar
1⅔ cups tomato juice
2 tablespoons powdered gelatin
fresh basil leaves, to garnish

FOR THE DRESSING
6 tablespoons extra virgin olive oil
2 tablespoons red wine vinegar
salt and ground black pepper

SERVES 6

1. Place the prepared red and yellow peppers skin side up under a hot broiler and cook until the skins are blackened. Transfer to a bowl and cover with a plate. Allow to cool.

2. Arrange the eggplant and zucchini slices on separate baking sheets. Brush them with a little oil and cook under the broiler, turning occasionally, until tender and golden.

3. Heat the remaining olive oil in a frying pan, and add the sliced onion, raisins, tomato paste and red wine vinegar. Cook gently until soft and syrupy. Let the mixture cool in the frying pan.

4. Line a 7½-cup terrine with plastic wrap (it helps to lightly oil the terrine first), leaving a little hanging over the sides.

5. Pour half the tomato juice into a saucepan, and sprinkle with the gelatin. Dissolve gently over low heat, stirring.

6. Place a layer of red peppers in the bottom of the terrine, and pour in enough of the tomato juice with gelatin to cover. Continue layering the eggplant, zucchini, yellow peppers and onion mixture, finishing with another layer of red peppers. Pour tomato juice over each layer of vegetables.

7. Add the remaining tomato juice to any left in the pan, and pour into the terrine. Give it a sharp tap, to disperse the juice. Cover the terrine and chill until set.

8. To make the dressing, whisk together the oil and vinegar, and season. Turn out the terrine and remove the plastic wrap. Serve in thick slices, drizzled with dressing. Garnish with basil leaves.

SALADS
AND VEGETABLES

*The climate of Greece has ensured that salads and
cold, cooked vegetable dishes have always been
popular. Cheese and yogurt are often mixed in
with salad vegetables, as in the very popular
Greek Salad or in the delicious Halloumi and
Grape Salad where the cheese is fried before being
added. Stuffed vegetables are greatly loved in
Greece, Turkey and the Middle East. Tomatoes,
eggplant, bell peppers, zucchini and onions are all
used as receptacles for a delicious variety of fillings.
Large leaves like grape leaves, spinach and cabbage
are stuffed with aromatic ingredients, packed in a
pan and gently cooked until all the flavors are
deliciously mingled.*

GREEK SALAD

*Anyone who has spent a holiday in Greece will have eaten a version of this salad — the Greeks'
equivalent to a mixed salad. Its success relies on using the freshest of ingredients, and a good olive oil.*

*1 small romaine lettuce, sliced
1 pound well-flavored tomatoes, cut
into eighths
1 cucumber, seeded and chopped
7 ounces feta cheese, crumbled
4 scallions, sliced
½ cup black olives, pitted
and halved*

FOR THE DRESSING
*6 tablespoons good olive oil
1½ tablespoons lemon juice
salt and ground black pepper*

SERVES 6

1 Put all the main salad
ingredients into a large bowl.
Whisk together the olive oil and
lemon juice, then season with salt
and pepper, and pour the dressing
on the salad. Mix well and
serve immediately.

SPICED EGGPLANT SALAD

*Serve this Middle-Eastern influenced salad with warm pita bread as an appetizer or to accompany a
main course rice pilaf.*

*2 small eggplant, sliced
5 tablespoons olive oil
¼ cup red wine vinegar
2 garlic cloves, crushed
1 tablespoon lemon juice
½ teaspoon ground cumin
½ teaspoon ground coriander
½ cucumber, thinly sliced
2 well-flavored tomatoes,
thinly sliced
2 tablespoons plain yogurt
salt and ground black pepper
chopped flat leaf parsley, to garnish*

SERVES 4

1 Preheat the broiler. Brush the
eggplant slices lightly with
some of the oil and cook under high
heat, turning once, until golden and
tender. Cut into quarters.

2 Mix together the remaining oil,
vinegar, garlic, lemon juice,
cumin and coriander. Season with salt
and pepper and mix thoroughly. Add
the warm eggplant, stir well and chill
for at least 2 hours. Add the cucumber
and tomatoes. Transfer to a serving
dish and spoon the yogurt on top.
Sprinkle with parsley.

CACIK

This refreshing yogurt dish is served all over the Eastern Mediterranean, whether as part of a mezze with marinated olives and pita bread, or as an accompaniment to meat dishes. Greek tzatziki is very similar.

1 small cucumber
1¼ cups thick plain yogurt
3 garlic cloves, crushed
2 tablespoons chopped fresh mint
2 tablespoons chopped fresh dill
or parsley
salt and ground black pepper
mint or parsley and dill, to garnish
olive oil, olives and pita bread,
to serve

SERVES 6

1 Finely chop the cucumber and layer in a colander with plenty of salt. Let sit for 30 minutes. Wash the cucumber in several changes of cold water and drain thoroughly. Pat dry on paper towels.

2 Mix together the yogurt, garlic and herbs and season with salt and pepper. Stir in the cucumber. Garnish with herbs, drizzle on a little olive oil and serve with olives and pita bread.

BROWN BEAN SALAD

Brown beans, sometimes called "ful medames," are widely used in Egyptian cooking, and are occasionally seen in health food shops here. Dried fava beans, black or red kidney beans make a good substitute.

1½ cups dried brown beans
3 thyme sprigs
2 bay leaves
1 onion, halved
4 garlic cloves, crushed
1½ teaspoons cumin seeds, crushed
3 scallions, finely chopped
6 tablespoons coarsely chopped
fresh parsley
4 teaspoons lemon juice
6 tablespoons olive oil
3 hard-boiled eggs, shelled and
coarsely chopped
1 dill pickle, roughly chopped
salt and ground black pepper

SERVES 6

1. Put the beans in a bowl with plenty of cold water and let soak overnight. Drain, transfer to a saucepan and cover with fresh water. Bring to a boil and boil rapidly for 10 minutes.

2. Reduce the heat and add the thyme, bay leaves and onion. Simmer very gently for about 1 hour until tender. Drain and discard the herbs and onion.

3. Mix together the garlic, cumin, scallions, parsley, lemon juice, oil and add a little salt and pepper. Pour on the beans and toss the ingredients lightly together.

4. Gently stir in the eggs and pickle and serve immediately.

COOK'S TIP
The cooking time for dried beans can vary considerably. They may need only 45 minutes, or a lot longer.

WARM FAVA BEAN AND FETA SALAD

This recipe is loosely based on a typical medley of fresh-tasting Greek salad ingredients — fava beans, tomatoes and feta cheese. It's lovely warm or cold as an appetizer or main course accompaniment.

2 pounds fava beans, shelled, or
12 ounces shelled frozen beans
4 tablespoons olive oil
6 ounces plum tomatoes, halved, or
quartered if large
4 garlic cloves, crushed
4 ounces firm feta cheese, cut
into chunks
3 tablespoons chopped fresh dill
12 black olives
salt and ground black pepper
chopped fresh dill, to garnish

SERVES 4–6

1 Cook the fresh or frozen fava beans in boiling, salted water until just tender. Drain and set aside.

2 Meanwhile, heat the oil in a heavy-based frying pan and add the tomatoes and garlic. Cook until the tomatoes are beginning to color.

3 Add the feta to the pan and toss the ingredients together for 1 minute. Mix with the drained beans, dill, olives and salt and pepper. Serve garnished with chopped dill.

HALLOUMI AND GRAPE SALAD

In Eastern Europe, firm salty halloumi cheese is often served fried for breakfast or supper. Feta cheese makes a good substitute in this recipe.

FOR THE DRESSING
4 tablespoons olive oil
1 tablespoon lemon juice
½ teaspoon sugar
salt and ground black pepper
1 tablespoon chopped fresh thyme
or dill

FOR THE SALAD
5 ounces mixed green salad leaves
3 ounces seedless green grapes
3 ounces seedless black grapes
9 ounces halloumi cheese
3 tablespoons olive oil
thyme leaves or dill, to garnish

SERVES 4

1 To make the dressing, mix together the olive oil, lemon juice and sugar. Season. Stir in the thyme or dill and set aside.

2 Toss together the salad greens and the green and black grapes, then transfer to a large serving plate.

3 Thinly slice the cheese. Heat the oil in a large frying pan. Add the cheese and fry briefly until turning golden on the underside. Turn the cheese with a spatula and cook the other side.

4 Arrange the cheese on the salad. Pour on the dressing and garnish with thyme or dill.

SIMPLE COOKED SALAD

A version of a popular Mediterranean recipe, this cooked salad is served as a side dish to accompany a main course. Make it the day before to enhance the flavor.

2 well-flavored tomatoes, quartered
2 onions, chopped
½ cucumber, halved lengthwise,
seeded and sliced
1 green bell pepper, halved, seeded
and chopped
2 tablespoons lemon juice
3 tablespoons olive oil
2 garlic cloves, crushed
2 tablespoons chopped fresh cilantro
salt and ground black pepper
sprigs of cilantro, to garnish

SERVES 4

1 Put the tomatoes, onions, cucumber and green bell pepper into a pan, add 4 tablespoons water and simmer for 5 minutes. Allow to cool.

2 Mix together the lemon juice, olive oil and garlic. Strain the vegetables, then transfer to a bowl. Pour on the dressing, season with salt and pepper and stir in the chopped cilantro. Serve immediately, garnished with cilantro, if you like.

SPICY CHICKPEA AND EGGPLANT STEW

This is a Lebanese dish, but similar recipes are found all over the Mediterranean.

3 large eggplant, cubed
1 cup chickpeas, soaked overnight
4 tablespoons olive oil
3 garlic cloves, chopped
2 large onions, chopped
½ teaspoon ground cumin
½ teaspoon ground cinnamon
2½ teaspoons ground coriander
3 x 14-ounce cans chopped tomatoes
salt and ground black pepper
cooked rice, to serve

FOR THE GARNISH
2 tablespoons olive oil
1 onion, sliced
1 garlic clove, sliced
sprigs of coriander

SERVES 4

1 Place the eggplant in a colander and sprinkle them with salt. Sit the colander in a bowl and leave for 30 minutes, to allow the bitter juices to escape. Rinse with cold water and dry on paper towels.

2 Drain the chickpeas and put in a pan with enough water to cover. Bring to a boil and simmer for 30 minutes, or until tender. Drain.

3 Heat the oil in a large pan. Add the garlic and onion and cook gently, until soft. Add the spices and cook, stirring, for a few seconds. Add the eggplant and stir to coat with the spices and onion. Cook for 5 minutes. Add the tomatoes and chickpeas and season with salt and pepper. Cover and simmer for 20 minutes.

4 To make the garnish, heat the oil in a frying pan and, when very hot, add the sliced onion and garlic. Fry until golden and crisp. Serve the stew with rice, topped with the onion and garlic and garnished with coriander.

POLPETTES

Delicious little fried morsels of potato and Greek feta cheese, flavored with dill and lemon juice.

1¼ pounds potatoes
4 ounces feta cheese
4 scallions, chopped
3 tablespoons chopped fresh dill
1 egg, beaten
1 tablespoon lemon juice
salt and ground black pepper
flour for dredging
3 tablespoons olive oil

SERVES 4

1 Boil the potatoes in their skins in lightly salted water until soft. Drain, then peel while still warm. Place in a bowl and mash. Crumble the feta cheese into the potatoes and add the scallions, dill, egg and lemon juice and season with salt and pepper. (The cheese is salty, so taste before you add salt.) Stir well.

2 Cover the mixture and chill until firm. Divide the mixture into walnut-size balls, then flatten them slightly. Dredge with flour. Heat the oil in a frying pan and fry the polpettes until golden brown on each side. Drain on paper towels and serve immediately.

SPICED TURNIPS WITH SPINACH AND TOMATOES

Sweet baby turnips, tender spinach and ripe tomatoes make tempting partners in this simple Eastern Mediterranean vegetable stew.

1 pound plum or other
well-flavored tomatoes
4 tablespoons olive oil
2 onions, sliced
1 pound baby turnips, peeled
1 teaspoon paprika
½ teaspoon caster sugar
4 tablespoons chopped fresh cilantro
1 pound fresh young spinach,
stalks removed
salt and ground black pepper

SERVES 6

1 Plunge the tomatoes into a bowl of boiling water for 30 seconds, then refresh in a bowl of cold water. Peel away the tomato skins and chop coarsely. Heat the olive oil in a large frying pan or sauté pan and fry the onion slices for about 5 minutes until golden.

2 Add the baby turnips, tomatoes and paprika to the pan with 4 tablespoons water and cook until the tomatoes are pulpy. Cover with a lid and continue cooking until the baby turnips have softened.

3 Stir in the sugar and cilantro, then add the spinach and a little salt and pepper and cook for another 2–3 minutes until the spinach has wilted. Serve warm or cold.

STUFFED TOMATOES AND PEPPERS

Colorful peppers and tomatoes make perfect containers for various meat and vegetable stuffings. This rice and herb version uses typically Greek ingredients.

VARIATION

Small eggplant or large zucchini also make good vegetables for stuffing. Halve and scoop out the centers of the vegetables, then oil the vegetable shells and bake for about 15 minutes. Chop the centers, fry for 2–3 minutes to soften and add to the stuffing mixture. Fill the eggplant or zucchini shells with the stuffing and bake as for the peppers and tomatoes.

2 large ripe tomatoes
1 green bell pepper
1 yellow or orange bell pepper
4 tablespoons olive oil, plus extra
for sprinkling
2 onions, chopped
2 garlic cloves, crushed
½ cup blanched almonds, chopped
scant ½ cup long grain rice, boiled
and drained
½ ounce mint, roughly chopped
½ ounce parsley, coarsely chopped
2 tablespoons golden raisins
3 tablespoons ground almonds
salt and ground black pepper
chopped mixed herbs, to garnish

SERVES 4

1 Preheat the oven to 375°F. Cut the tomatoes in half and scoop out the pulp and seeds using a teaspoon. Leave the tomatoes to drain on paper towels with cut sides down. Coarsely chop the tomato pulp and seeds and set aside.

2 Halve the peppers, leaving the cores intact. Scoop out the seeds. Brush the peppers with 1 tablespoon of the oil and bake on a baking sheet for 15 minutes. Place the peppers and tomatoes in a shallow ovenproof dish and season with salt and pepper.

3 Fry the onions in the remaining oil for 5 minutes. Add the garlic and chopped almonds and fry for another minute.

4   Remove the pan from the heat and stir in the rice, chopped tomatoes, mint, parsley and golden raisins. Season well with salt and pepper and spoon the mixture into the tomatoes and peppers.

5   Pour ⅔ cup boiling water around the tomatoes and peppers and bake, uncovered, for 20 minutes. Scatter with the ground almonds and sprinkle with a little extra olive oil. Return to the oven and bake for 20 minutes more, or until turning golden. Serve garnished with fresh herbs.

OKRA WITH CORIANDER AND TOMATOES

Okra is frequently combined with tomatoes and mild spices in various parts of the Mediterranean. Buy okra only if it is soft and velvety, not dry and shriveled.

1 pound tomatoes or 14-ounce can
chopped tomatoes
1 pound fresh okra
3 tablespoons olive oil
2 onions, thinly sliced
2 teaspoons coriander seeds, crushed
3 garlic cloves, crushed
½ teaspoon sugar
finely grated rind and juice
of 1 lemon
salt and ground black pepper

SERVES 4

1 If using fresh tomatoes, plunge them into boiling water for 30 seconds, then refresh in cold water. Peel away the skins and chop.

2 Trim off any stalks from the okra and keep whole. Heat the oil in a sauté pan and fry the onions and coriander for 3–4 minutes until beginning to color.

3 Add the okra and garlic and fry for 1 minute. Gently stir in the tomatoes and sugar and simmer gently for about 20 minutes, until the okra is tender, stirring once or twice. Stir in the lemon rind and juice and add salt and pepper to taste, adding a little more sugar if necessary. Serve warm or cold.

STUFFED PEPPERS

Couscous is a form of semolina, and is used extensively in the Middle East. It makes a good basis for a stuffing, combined with other ingredients.

6 bell peppers
2 tablespoons butter
1 onion, finely chopped
1 teaspoon olive oil
½ teaspoon salt
1 cup couscous
2 tablespoons raisins
2 tablespoons chopped fresh mint
1 egg yolk
salt and ground black pepper
mint leaves, to garnish

SERVES 4

1 Preheat the oven to 400°F. Carefully slit each pepper and remove the core and seeds. Melt the butter in a small pan and add the onion. Cook until soft.

2 To cook the couscous, bring 1 cup water to the boil. Add the olive oil and the salt, then remove the pan from the heat and add the couscous. Stir and let stand, covered, for about 5 minutes. Stir in the cooked onion, raisins and mint, then season well with salt and pepper. Stir in the egg yolk.

3 Using a teaspoon, fill the peppers with the couscous mixture to only about three-quarters full, as the couscous will swell when cooked further. Place in a lightly oiled ovenproof dish and bake, uncovered, for about 20 minutes until tender. Serve hot or cold, garnished with the mint leaves.

STUFFED VINE LEAVES WITH GARLIC YOGURT

An old Greek recipe which comes in many guises. This meatless version is highly flavored with fresh herbs, lemon and a little chili.

8-ounce packet preserved vine leaves
1 onion, finely chopped
½ bunch of scallions, trimmed and
finely chopped
4 tablespoons chopped fresh parsley
10 large mint sprigs, chopped
finely grated rind of 1 lemon
½ teaspoon crushed dried chilies
1½ teaspoons fennel seeds, crushed
scant 1 cup long grain rice
½ cup olive oil
⅔ cup thick plain yogurt
2 garlic cloves, crushed
salt
lemon wedges and mint leaves,
to garnish (optional)

SERVES 6

1 Rinse the vine leaves in plenty of cold water. Put in a bowl, cover with boiling water and let sit for 10 minutes. Drain thoroughly.

2 Mix together the onion, scallions, parsley, mint, lemon, chili, fennel, rice and 1½ tablespoons of the olive oil. Mix thoroughly and season with salt.

3 Place a vine leaf, veined side facing upwards, on a work surface and cut off any stalk. Place a heaped teaspoonful of the rice mixture near the stalk end of the leaf.

4 Fold the stalk end of the leaf over the rice filling, then fold over the sides and carefully roll up into a neat cigar shape.

5 Repeat with the remaining filling to make about 28 stuffed leaves. If some of the vine leaves are quite small, use two and patch them together to make parcels of the same size.

6 Place any remaining leaves in the base of a large heavy-based saucepan. Pack the stuffed leaves in a single layer in the pan. Spoon on the remaining oil, then add about 1¼ cups boiling water.

COOK'S TIP

To check that the rice is cooked, lift out one stuffed leaf and cut in half. The rice should have expanded and softened to make a firm parcel. If necessary, cook the stuffed leaves a little longer, adding boiling water if the pan is becoming dry.

7 Place a small plate over the leaves to keep them submerged in the water. Cover the pan and cook on a very low heat for 45 minutes.

8 Mix together the yogurt and garlic and put in a small serving dish. Transfer the stuffed leaves to a serving plate and garnish with lemon wedges and mint, if you like. Serve with the garlic yogurt.

FISH
AND SEAFOOD

The Mediterranean provides a rich source
of fish, so that recipes for using the many different
types are abundant. Plaki is a well-loved
example, perfect for fish such as cod, gray mullet
and bass, which absorb all the wonderful flavors of
the other ingredients. Middle Eastern fish
dishes emphasize the accompanying sauce –
the choice of fish being the pick
of the catch. Baked Fish with Tahini Sauce – a
simple blend of tahini with olive oil and lemon
juice – is classic. Squid and octopus both play an
important role in Greek cuisine. Squid, from the
tiniest, which are lovely seared in olive oil with
garlic and herbs, to the biggest specimens, rich
with stuffings, typify Greek culinary techniques.

JUMBO SHRIMP WITH PIQUANT TOMATO SAUCE

This spicy sauce is served with fish and seafood. Its main ingredients are sweet peppers, tomatoes, garlic and almonds.

❧❧

24 raw jumbo shrimp
2–3 tablespoons olive oil
flat leaf parsley, to garnish
lemon wedges, to serve

FOR THE SAUCE
2 well-flavored tomatoes
4 tablespoons olive oil
1 onion, chopped
4 garlic cloves, chopped
1 canned pimiento, chopped
½ teaspoon dried chili flakes
or powder
5 tablespoons fish stock
2 tablespoons white wine
10 blanched almonds
1 tablespoon red wine vinegar
salt

SERVES 4

1 To make the sauce, immerse the tomatoes in boiling water for about 30 seconds, then refresh them under cold water. Peel away the skins and coarsely chop the flesh.

2 Heat 2 tablespoons of the oil in a pan, add the onion and 3 of the garlic cloves and cook until soft. Add the pimiento, tomatoes, chili, fish stock and wine, then cover and simmer for 30 minutes.

3 Toast the almonds under the broiler until golden. Transfer to a blender or food processor and grind coarsely. Add the remaining 2 tablespoons of oil, the vinegar and the last garlic clove and process until evenly combined. Add the tomato and pimiento sauce and process until smooth. Season with salt.

4 Remove the heads from the shrimp leaving them otherwise unshelled and, with a sharp knife, slit each one down the back and remove the dark vein. Rinse and pat dry on paper towels. Preheat the broiler. Toss the shrimp in olive oil, then spread out in the broiler pan. Broil for about 2–3 minutes on each side, until pink. Arrange on a serving platter with the lemon wedges, and the sauce in a small bowl. Serve immediately, garnished with parsley.

GRILLED SEA BASS WITH FENNEL

This simple dish brings out the full flavor of the fish. Traditionally fennel twigs are used but, as they are hard to find, this recipe uses fennel seeds.

*1 sea bass, weighing
4–4½ pounds, cleaned
4–6 tablespoons olive oil
2–3 teaspoons fennel seeds
2 large fennel bulbs, trimmed and
thinly sliced (reserve any fronds)
4 tablespoons Pernod
salt and ground black pepper*

SERVES 6–8

1 With a sharp knife, make three or four deep cuts in both sides of the fish. Brush the fish with olive oil and season with salt and pepper. Sprinkle the fennel seeds in the stomach cavity and in the cuts. Set aside while you cook the fennel.

2 Preheat the broiler. Put the slices of fennel in a flameproof dish or on the broiler rack and brush with oil. Broil for 4 minutes on each side until tender. Transfer to a large platter.

3 Place the fish on the oiled broiler rack and position about 4–5 inches away from the heat. Cook for 10–12 minutes on each side, brushing with oil occasionally.

4 Transfer the fish to the platter on top of the fennel. Garnish with fennel fronds. Heat the Pernod in a small pan, light it and pour it, flaming, over the fish. Serve at once.

COD PLAKI

Greece has so much coastline, it's no wonder that fish is popular all over the country. Generally, it is treated very simply, but this recipe is a little more involved, baking the fish with onions and tomatoes.

1¼ cups olive oil
2 onions, thinly sliced
3 large well-flavored tomatoes,
coarsely chopped
3 garlic cloves, thinly sliced
1 teaspoon sugar
1 teaspoon chopped fresh dill
1 teaspoon chopped fresh mint
1 teaspoon chopped fresh celery leaves
1 tablespoon chopped fresh parsley
6 cod steaks
juice of 1 lemon
salt and ground black pepper
extra dill, mint or parsley, to garnish

SERVES 6

1 Heat the oil in a large sauté pan or flameproof dish. Add the onions and cook until pale golden. Add the tomatoes, garlic, sugar, dill, mint, celery leaves and parsley with 1¼ cups water. Season with salt and pepper, then simmer, uncovered, for 25 minutes, until the liquid has reduced by one-third.

2 Add the fish steaks and cook gently for 10–12 minutes, until the fish is just cooked. Remove from the heat and add the lemon juice (*left*). Cover and let stand for about 20 minutes before serving. Arrange the cod in a dish and spoon the sauce on. Garnish with herbs and serve warm or cold.

STUFFED SQUID

This Greek delicacy is best made with large squid as they are less awkward to stuff. If you have to make do with small squid, buy about 1 pound.

FOR THE STUFFING
2 tablespoons olive oil
1 large onion, finely chopped
2 garlic cloves, crushed
1 cup fresh bread crumbs
4 tablespoons chopped fresh parsley
4 ounces halloumi cheese, grated
salt and ground black pepper

TO FINISH
4 squid tubes, each about
7 inches long
2 pounds ripe tomatoes
3 tablespoons olive oil
1 large onion, chopped
1 teaspoon sugar
½ cup dry white wine
several rosemary sprigs
toasted pine nuts and flat leaf parsley,
to garnish

SERVES 4

1 To make the stuffing, heat the oil in a frying pan and fry the onion for 3 minutes. Remove the pan from the heat and add the garlic, bread crumbs, parsley, cheese and a little salt and pepper. Stir until thoroughly blended.

2 Dry the squid tubes on paper towels and fill with the prepared stuffing using a teaspoon. Secure the ends of the squid tubes with wooden toothpicks.

VARIATION
If you would prefer a less rich filling, halve the quantity of cheese and bread crumbs in the stuffing and add 8 ounces cooked spinach.

3 Plunge the tomatoes into boiling water for 30 seconds, then refresh in cold water. Peel away the skins and chop coarsely.

4 Heat the oil in a frying pan or sauté pan. Add the squid and fry on all sides. Remove from the pan.

5 Add the onion to the pan and fry gently for 3 minutes. Stir in the tomatoes, sugar and wine and cook rapidly until the mixture becomes thick and pulpy.

6 Return the squid to the pan with the rosemary. Cover and cook gently for 30 minutes. Slice the squid and serve on individual plates with the sauce. Scatter on the pine nuts and garnish with parsley.

PAN-FRIED RED MULLET WITH BASIL AND CITRUS

Red mullet is popular all over the Mediterranean. This recipe combines it with oranges and lemons, which grow in abundance.

4 red mullet, about 8 ounces
each, filleted
6 tablespoons olive oil
10 peppercorns, crushed
2 oranges, one peeled and sliced and
one squeezed
1 lemon
2 tablespoons flour
1 tablespoon butter
2 drained canned anchovies, chopped
4 tablespoons shredded fresh basil
salt and ground black pepper

SERVES 4

1 Place the fish fillets in a shallow dish in a single layer. Pour on the olive oil and sprinkle with the crushed peppercorns. Lay the orange slices on top of the fish. Cover the dish, and allow to marinate in the fridge for at least 4 hours.

2 Halve the lemon. Remove the skin and pith from one half using a small sharp knife, and slice thinly. Squeeze the juice from the other half.

3 Lift the fish out of the marinade, and pat dry on paper towels. Reserve the marinade and orange slices. Season the fish with salt and pepper and dust lightly with flour.

4 Heat 3 tablespoons of the marinade in a frying pan. Add the fish and fry for 2 minutes on each side. Remove from the pan and keep warm. Discard the marinade that is left in the pan.

5 Melt the butter in the pan with any of the remaining original marinade. Add the anchovies and cook until completely softened.

6 Stir in the orange and lemon juice, then check the seasoning and simmer until slightly reduced. Stir in the basil. Pour the sauce on the fish and garnish with the reserved orange slices and the lemon slices.

COOK'S TIP
If you prefer, use other fish fillets for this dish, such as red snapper, lemon sole, haddock or hake.

OCTOPUS AND RED WINE STEW

Unless you're happy to clean and prepare octopus for this Greek dish, buy one that's ready for cooking.

2 pounds prepared octopus
1 pound onions, sliced
2 bay leaves
1 pound ripe tomatoes
4 tablespoons olive oil
4 garlic cloves, crushed
1 teaspoon sugar
1 tablespoon chopped fresh oregano
or rosemary
2 tablespoons chopped fresh parsley
⅔ cup red wine
2 tablespoons red wine vinegar
chopped fresh herbs, to garnish
warm bread and pine nuts, to serve

SERVES 4

1 Put the octopus in a saucepan of gently simmering water with a quarter of the onions and the bay leaves. Cook gently for 1 hour.

2 While the octopus is cooking, plunge the tomatoes into boiling water for 30 seconds, then refresh in cold water. Peel away the skins and chop coarsely.

3 Drain the octopus and, using a sharp knife, cut it into bite-size pieces. Discard the head.

4 Heat the oil in a saucepan and fry the octopus, the remaining onions and the garlic for 3 minutes. Add the tomatoes, sugar, oregano or rosemary, parsley, wine and vinegar and cook, stirring, for 5 minutes until pulpy.

5 Cover the pan and cook over the lowest possible heat for about 1½ hours until the sauce is thickened and the octopus is tender. Garnish with fresh herbs and serve with warm bread, and pine nuts to scatter on top.

VARIATION
Use white wine instead of red and stir in ½ cup coarsely chopped black olives before serving.

FRESH TUNA AND TOMATO STEW

A deliciously simple dish that relies on good basic ingredients. Serve with plain boiled rice and a green vegetable.

12 baby onions, peeled
2 pounds ripe tomatoes
1½ pounds fresh tuna
3 tablespoons olive oil
2 garlic cloves, crushed
3 tablespoons chopped fresh herbs
2 bay leaves
½ teaspoon sugar
2 tablespoons sun-dried tomato paste
⅔ cup dry white wine
salt and ground black pepper
baby zucchini and fresh herbs,
to garnish

SERVES 4

VARIATION
Two large mackerel make a more readily available alternative to the tuna. Fillet them and cut into chunks or simply lay the whole fish on the sauce and cook, covered with a lid until the mackerel is cooked through. Sage, rosemary or oregano all go extremely well with this dish. Choose whichever you prefer, or use a mixture of one or two.

1 | Leave the onions whole and cook in a pan of boiling water for 4–5 minutes until softened. Drain.

2 | Plunge the tomatoes into boiling water for 30 seconds, then refresh in cold water. Peel away the skins and chop coarsely.

4 | Add the onions, garlic, tomatoes, chopped herbs, bay leaves, sugar, tomato paste and wine and bring to a boil, breaking up the tomatoes with a wooden spoon.

5 | Reduce the heat and simmer gently for 5 minutes. Return the fish to the pan and cook for another 5 minutes. Season, and serve hot, garnished with baby zucchini and fresh herbs.

3 | Cut the tuna into 1-inch chunks. Heat the oil in a large frying or sauté pan and quickly fry the tuna until browned. Drain.

BAKED FISH WITH TAHINI SAUCE

This recipe evokes all the color and rich flavors of Eastern Mediterranean cuisine. Choose any whole white fish, such as sea bass, hake, bream or snapper.

1 whole fish, about 2½ pounds, scaled and cleaned
2 teaspoons coriander seeds
4 garlic cloves, sliced
2 teaspoons harissa sauce
6 tablespoons olive oil
6 plum tomatoes, sliced
1 mild onion, sliced
3 preserved lemons or 1 fresh lemon
plenty of fresh herbs, such as bay leaves, thyme and rosemary
salt and ground black pepper

FOR THE SAUCE
⅓ cup light tahini
juice of 1 lemon
1 garlic clove, crushed
3 tablespoons finely chopped fresh parsley or cilantro
extra herbs, to garnish

SERVES 4

1 Preheat the oven to 400°F. Grease the base and sides of a large shallow ovenproof dish or roasting pan.

2 Slash the fish diagonally on both sides with a sharp knife. Finely crush the coriander seeds and garlic with a pestle and mortar. Mix with the harissa sauce and about 4 tablespoons of the olive oil.

3 Spread a little of the harissa, coriander and garlic paste inside the cavity of the fish. Spread the remainder over each side of the fish and set aside.

4 Scatter the tomatoes, onion and preserved or fresh lemon into the dish. (Thinly slice the lemon if using fresh.) Sprinkle with the remaining oil and season with salt and pepper. Lay the fish on top and tuck plenty of herbs around it.

5 Bake, uncovered, for about 25 minutes, or until the fish has turned opaque – test by piercing the thickest part with a knife.

6 Meanwhile, make the sauce. Put the tahini, lemon juice, garlic and parsley or cilantro in a small saucepan with ½ cup water and add a little salt and pepper. Cook gently until smooth and heated through. Serve in a separate dish.

COOK'S TIP
If you can't get a suitable large fish, use small whole fish such as red snapper or even cod or haddock steaks. Remember to reduce the cooking time slightly.

POULTRY AND MEAT

*Since meat is scarcer than fish in the
countries of the Eastern Mediterranean, the
traditional recipes are designed to make a little go
a long way, as in the classic Greek Moussaka, for
which ground lamb is layered with eggplant, then
topped with cheese sauce and in Lamb Pilau,
where rice gives substance to the dish. Spices, nuts
and dried fruits are often mixed with the meat to
make delicious fillings for little parcels of filo, such
as Chicken and Apricot Filo Pie. These versatile
dishes are great when entertaining a large group of
friends.*

DUCK BREASTS WITH A WALNUT AND POMEGRANATE SAUCE

—

This is an extremely exotic sweet and sour dish which originally came from Persia.

4 tablespoons olive oil
2 onions, very thinly sliced
½ teaspoon ground turmeric
3½ cups walnuts, coarsely chopped
4 cups duck or chicken stock
6 pomegranates
2 tablespoons sugar
4 tablespoons lemon juice
4 duck breasts, about 8 ounces each
salt and ground black pepper

SERVES 6

COOK'S TIP
Choose pomegranates with shiny, brightly colored skins. The juice stains, so be careful when cutting them. Only the seeds are used in cooking, the pith is discarded.

1 Heat half the oil in a frying pan. Add the onions and turmeric, and cook gently until soft. Transfer to a pan, add the walnuts and stock, then season with salt and pepper. Stir, then bring to a boil and simmer the mixture, uncovered, for 20 minutes.

2 Cut the pomegranates in half and scoop out the seeds into a bowl. Reserve the seeds of one pomegranate. Transfer the remaining seeds to a blender or food processor, and process to break them up. Put through a strainer to extract the juice, and stir in the sugar and lemon juice.

3 Score the skin of the duck breasts in a lattice fashion with a sharp knife. Heat the remaining oil in a frying pan or char grill and place the duck breasts in it, skin side down.

4 Cook gently for 10 minutes, pouring off the fat from time to time, until the skin is dark golden and crisp. Turn them over and cook for another 3–4 minutes. Transfer to a plate and allow to rest.

5 Deglaze the frying pan or char grill with the pomegranate juice mixture, stirring with a wooden spoon, then add the walnut and stock mixture and simmer for 15 minutes until the sauce has thickened slightly. Serve the duck breasts sliced, drizzled with a little sauce, and garnished with the reserved pomegranate seeds. Serve the remaining sauce separately.

CIRCASSIAN CHICKEN

This is a Turkish dish, which is popular all over the Middle East. The chicken is poached and served cold with a flavorful walnut sauce.

3½-pound chicken
2 onions, quartered
1 carrot, sliced
1 celery stalk, trimmed and sliced
6 peppercorns
3 slices bread, crusts removed
2 garlic cloves, coarsely chopped
3½ cups chopped walnuts
1 tablespoon walnut oil
salt and ground black pepper
chopped walnuts and paprika,
to garnish

SERVES 6

1 Place the chicken in a large pan, with the onions, carrot, celery and peppercorns. Add enough water to cover, and bring to a boil. Simmer for about 1 hour, uncovered, until the chicken is tender. Allow to cool in the stock. Drain the chicken, reserving the stock.

2 Tear up the bread and soak in 6 tablespoons of the chicken stock. Transfer to a blender or food processor, with the garlic and walnuts, and add 1 cup of the remaining stock. Process until smooth, then transfer to a pan.

3 Over low heat, gradually add more chicken stock to the sauce, stirring constantly, until it is a thick pouring consistency. Season with salt and pepper, remove from the heat and let cool in the pan. Skin and bone the chicken, and cut into bite-size chunks.

4 Place in a bowl and add a little of the saucc. Stir to coat the chicken, then arrange on a serving dish. Spoon the remaining sauce over the chicken, and drizzle with the walnut oil. Sprinkle with walnuts and paprika and serve at once.

CHICKEN WITH LEMONS AND OLIVES

Preserved lemons and limes are frequently used in Mediterranean cookery. They have a gentle flavor which can enhance all kinds of meat and fish dishes.

½ teaspoon ground cinnamon
½ teaspoon ground turmeric
3½-pound chicken
2 tablespoons olive oil
1 large onion, thinly sliced
2-inch piece fresh ginger
root, grated
2½ cups chicken stock
2 preserved lemons or limes, or fresh,
cut into wedges
½ cup pitted brown olives
1 tablespoon honey
4 tablespoons chopped fresh cilantro
salt and ground black pepper
cilantro sprigs, to garnish

SERVES 4

1 Preheat the oven to 375°F. Mix the ground cinnamon and turmeric in a small bowl with a little salt and pepper and rub all over the chicken skin to give an even coating.

2 Heat the oil in a large sauté or shallow frying pan and fry the chicken on all sides until it turns golden. Transfer the chicken to an ovenproof dish.

3 Add the sliced onion to the pan and fry for 3 minutes. Stir in the grated ginger and the chicken stock and bring just to a boil. Pour on the chicken, cover with a lid and bake in the oven for 30 minutes.

4 Remove the chicken from the oven and add the lemons or limes, brown olives and honey. Bake, uncovered, for another 45 minutes until the chicken is tender.

5 Stir in the cilantro and season to taste. Garnish with cilantro sprigs and serve immediately.

CHICKEN AND APRICOT FILO PIE

The filling for this pie has a Middle Eastern flavor — chopped chicken combined with apricots, bulgur wheat, nuts and spices.

½ cup bulgur wheat
6 tablespoons butter
1 onion, chopped
1 pound chopped chicken
¼ cup ready-to-eat dried apricots, finely chopped
¼ cup blanched almonds, chopped
1 teaspoon ground cinnamon
½ teaspoon ground allspice
¼ cup strained plain yogurt
1 tablespoon snipped fresh chives
2 tablespoons chopped fresh parsley
6 large sheets filo pastry
salt and ground black pepper
chives, to garnish

SERVES 6

1 Preheat the oven to 400°F. Put the bulgur wheat in a bowl with ½ cup boiling water. Soak for 5–10 minutes, until the water is absorbed.

2 Heat 2 tablespoons of the butter in a pan, and gently fry the onion and chicken until pale golden.

3 Stir in the apricots, almonds and bulgur wheat and cook for 2 minutes more. Remove from the heat and stir in the cinnamon, allspice, yogurt, chives and parsley. Season to taste with salt and pepper.

4 Melt the remaining butter. Unroll the filo pastry and cut into 10-inch circles. Keep the pastry circles covered with a clean, damp dish towel to prevent drying.

5 Line a 9-inch loose-based quiche pan with three of the pastry circles, brushing each one with butter as you layer them. Spoon in the chicken mixture, cover with three more pastry rounds, brushed with melted butter as before.

6 Crumple the remaining circles and place them on top of the pie, then brush on any remaining melted butter. Bake the pie for about 30 minutes, until the pastry is golden brown and crisp. Serve Chicken and Apricot Filo Pie hot or cold, cut in wedges and garnished with chives.

AFELIA

This lightly-spiced pork stew makes a really delicious supper dish served simply, as it would be in Cyprus, with warmed bread, a leafy salad and a few olives.

3   Preheat the oven to 325°F. Heat 2 tablespoons of the oil in a frying pan over high heat. Brown the meat quickly, then transfer to an ovenproof dish.

1½-pound pork fillet, boneless leg or
chump steaks
4 teaspoons coriander seeds
½ teaspoon caster sugar
3 tablespoons olive oil
2 large onions, sliced
1¼ cups red wine
salt and ground black pepper
fresh cilantro, to garnish

SERVES 4

1   Cut the pork into small chunks, discarding any excess fat. Crush the coriander seeds with a pestle and mortar until fairly finely ground.

2   Mix the coriander seeds with the sugar and salt and pepper and rub all over the meat. Allow to marinate for up to 4 hours.

4   Add the remaining oil to the pan and fry the onions until beginning to color. Stir in the wine and a little salt and pepper and bring just to a boil.

5   Pour the onion and wine mixture over the meat and cover with a lid. Bake for 1 hour, or until the meat is very tender. Serve scattered with fresh cilantro.

COOK'S TIP
A coffee grinder can also be used to grind the coriander seeds.
Alternatively, use 1 tablespoon ground coriander.

LAMB PILAU

Here we have a delicious combination of rice, lamb, spices, nuts and fruit — a typical Middle Eastern dish.

*3 tablespoons butter
1 large onion, finely chopped
1 pound lamb fillet, cut into
small cubes
½ teaspoon ground cinnamon
2 tablespoons tomato paste
3 tablespoons chopped fresh parsley
½ cup ready-to-eat dried
apricots, halved
¾ cup pistachio nuts
1 pound long grain rice, rinsed
salt and ground black pepper
flat leaf parsley, to garnish*

SERVES 4

1   Heat the butter in a large heavy-based pan. Add the onion and cook until soft and golden. Add the cubed lamb and brown on all sides. Add the cinnamon and season with salt and pepper. Cover and cook gently for 10 minutes.

2   Add the tomato paste and enough water to cover the meat. Stir in the parsley, bring to a boil, cover and simmer very gently for 1½ hours, until the meat is tender. Chop the pistachio nuts.

3   Add enough water to the pan to measure about 2½ cups liquid. Add the apricots, pistachio nuts and rice, bring to a boil, cover tightly and simmer for about 20 minutes, until the rice is cooked. (You may need to add a little more water, if necessary.) Transfer to a warmed serving dish and garnish with parsley before serving.

GREEK LAMB SAUSAGES WITH TOMATO SAUCE

The Greek name for these sausages is soudzoukakia. They are more like elongated meatballs than the type of sausage we are accustomed to. Passata is strained tomato, which can be bought in cartons or jars.

1 cup fresh bread crumbs
⅔ cup milk
1½ pounds ground lamb
2 tablespoons grated onion
3 garlic cloves, crushed
2 teaspoons ground cumin
2 tablespoons chopped fresh parsley
flour for dusting
olive oil for frying
2½ cups passata
1 teaspoon sugar
2 bay leaves
1 small onion, peeled
salt and ground black pepper
flat leaf parsley, to garnish

SERVES 4

1 Mix together the bread crumbs and milk. Add the lamb, onion, garlic, cumin and parsley and season with salt and pepper.

2 Shape the mixture with your hands into little fat sausages, about 2 inches long, and roll them in flour. Heat about 4 tablespoons olive oil in a frying pan.

3 Fry the sausages for about 8 minutes, turning them until evenly browned. Remove and place on paper towels to drain.

4 Put the passata, sugar, bay leaves and whole onion in a pan and simmer for 20 minutes. Add the sausages and cook for 10 minutes more. Serve garnished with parsley.

MOUSSAKA

Like many popular classics, a real moussaka bears little resemblance to the imitations experienced in many Greek tourist resorts. This one is mildly spiced, moist but not dripping in grease, and encased in a golden baked crust.

2 pounds eggplant
½ cup olive oil
2 large tomatoes
2 large onions, sliced
1 pound ground lamb
¼ teaspoon ground cinnamon
¼ teaspoon ground allspice
2 tablespoons tomato paste
3 tablespoons chopped fresh parsley
½ cup dry white wine
salt and ground black pepper

FOR THE SAUCE
4 tablespoons butter
½ cup flour
2½ cups milk
¼ teaspoon grated nutmeg
⅓ cup grated Parmesan cheese
3 tablespoons toasted bread crumbs

SERVES 6

1 Cut the eggplant into ¼-inch thick slices. Layer the slices in a colander, sprinkling each layer with plenty of salt. Let stand for 30 minutes.

2 Rinse the eggplant in several changes of cold water. Squeeze gently with your fingers to remove the excess water, then pat them dry on paper towels.

3 Heat some of the oil in a large frying pan. Fry the eggplant slices in batches until golden on both sides, adding more oil when necessary. Let the fried eggplant slices drain on paper towels.

4 Plunge the tomatoes into boiling water for 30 seconds, then refresh in cold water. Peel away the skins and chop coarsely.

5 Preheat the oven to 350°F. Heat 2 tablespoons oil in a saucepan. Add the onions and lamb and fry gently for 5 minutes, stirring and breaking up the lamb with a wooden spoon.

VARIATION
Sliced and sautéed zucchini or potatoes can be used instead of the eggplant in this dish.

6 Add the tomatoes, cinnamon, allspice, tomato paste, parsley, wine and pepper and bring to a boil. Reduce the heat, cover with a lid and simmer gently for 15 minutes.

7 Spoon alternate layers of the eggplant and meat mixture into a shallow ovenproof dish, finishing with a layer of eggplant.

8 To make the sauce, melt the butter in a small pan and stir in the flour. Cook, stirring, for 1 minute. Remove from the heat and gradually blend in the milk. Return to the heat and cook, stirring, for 2 minutes, until thickened. Add the nutmeg, cheese and salt and pepper. Pour the sauce on the eggplant and sprinkle with the bread crumbs. Bake for 45 minutes until golden. Serve hot, sprinkled with extra black pepper, if you like.

SKEWERED LAMB WITH CILANTRO YOGURT

Although lamb is the most commonly used meat for Turkish kebabs, lean beef or pork work equally well.
For color you can alternate pieces of pepper, lemon or onions, although this is not traditional.

2 pounds lean boneless lamb
1 large onion, grated
3 bay leaves
5 thyme or rosemary sprigs
grated rind and juice of
1 lemon
½ teaspoon sugar
⅓ cup olive oil
salt and ground black pepper
sprigs of rosemary, to garnish
broiled lemon wedges, to serve

FOR THE CORIANDER YOGURT
⅔ cup thick plain yogurt
1 tablespoon chopped fresh mint
1 tablespoon chopped
fresh cilantro
2 teaspoons grated onion

SERVES 4

1 To make the cilantro yogurt, mix together the yogurt, mint, cilantro and grated onion and transfer to a small serving dish.

2 To make the kebabs, cut the lamb into small chunks and put in a bowl. Mix together the grated onion, herbs, lemon rind and juice, sugar and oil, then add salt and pepper and pour on the lamb.

3 Mix the ingredients together and let marinate in the fridge for several hours or overnight.

4 Drain the meat and thread onto skewers. Arrange on a broiler rack and cook under a preheated broiler for about 10 minutes until browned, turning occasionally. Transfer to a plate and garnish with rosemary. Serve with the broiled lemon wedges and the cilantro yogurt.

COOK'S TIP
Cover the tips of wooden skewers with foil so they don't char.

KLEFTIKO

For this Greek recipe, marinated lamb steaks or chops are slow-cooked to develop an unbeatable, meltingly tender flavor. The dish is sealed, like a pie, with a flour dough lid to trap succulence and flavor, although a tight-fitting foil cover, if less attractive, will serve equally well.

juice of 1 lemon
1 tablespoon chopped fresh oregano
4 lamb leg steaks or chump chops
with bones
2 tablespoons olive oil
2 large onions, thinly sliced
2 bay leaves
⅔ cup dry white wine
2 cups flour
salt and ground black pepper

SERVES 4

COOK'S TIP
They are not absolutely essential for this dish, but lamb steaks or chops with bones will provide lots of additional flavor. Boiled potatoes make a delicious accompaniment.

1 Mix together the lemon juice, oregano and salt and pepper, and brush over both sides of the lamb steaks or chops. Allow to marinate for at least 4 hours or overnight.

2 Preheat the oven to 325°F. Drain the lamb, reserving the marinade, and dry the lamb with paper towels. Heat the olive oil in a large frying pan or sauté pan and fry the lamb over high heat until browned on both sides.

3 Transfer the lamb to a shallow pie dish. Scatter the sliced onions and bay leaves around the lamb, then pour on the white wine and the reserved marinade.

4 Mix the flour with enough water to make a firm dough. Moisten the rim of the pie dish. Roll out the dough on a floured surface and use to cover the dish so that it is tightly sealed.

5 Bake for 2 hours, then break away the dough crust and serve the lamb hot with boiled potatoes.

GRAINS
AND PULSES

Chick peas are probably the most popular
of the Eastern Mediterranean pulses and form the
basis of creamy pastes, such as the much-loved
Hummus bi Tahini. Rice is a common part of the
meals of this region served either plain boiled or
heavily spiced and mixed with numerous herbs,
dried fruits, nuts and vegetables, such as Pilaf
with Saffron and Pickled Walnuts. Bread is
produced in many different varieties and on special
occasions festive breads are popular, the most
elaborate being the braided Greek Easter Bread,
flavored with nuts and fruit and adorned with
hard-cooked eggs that are dyed red. According to
legend, the eggs will keep people who eat them
safe from harm.

HUMMUS BI TAHINA

Blending chickpeas with garlic and oil makes a surprisingly creamy purée that is delicious as part of a Turkish-style mezze, or as a dip with vegetables. Leftovers make a good sandwich filler.

¾ *cup dried chickpeas*
juice of 2 lemons
2 garlic cloves, sliced
2 tablespoons olive oil
pinch of cayenne pepper
⅔ *cup tahini paste*
salt and ground black pepper
extra olive oil and cayenne pepper
for sprinkling
flat leaf parsley, to garnish

SERVES 4–6

1 Put the chickpeas in a bowl with plenty of cold water and let soak overnight.

2 Drain the chickpeas and cover with fresh water in a saucepan. Bring to a boil and boil rapidly for 10 minutes. Reduce the heat and simmer gently for about 1 hour until soft. Drain.

3 Process the chickpeas in a food processor to a smooth purée. Add the lemon juice, garlic, olive oil, cayenne pepper and tahini and blend until creamy, scraping the mixture down from the sides of the bowl.

4 Season the purée with salt and pepper and transfer to a serving dish. Sprinkle with oil and cayenne pepper and serve garnished with a few parsley sprigs.

COOK'S TIP
For convenience, canned chickpeas can be used instead. Allow two 14-ounce cans and drain them thoroughly. Tahini paste can now be purchased from most supermarkets or health-food stores.

SPICED RICE AND LENTILS

*Lentils are cooked with spices in many ways in the Middle East and two important staples come together
in this dish, which can be served hot or cold.*

1½ cups large brown lentils, soaked
overnight in water
2 large onions
3 tablespoons olive oil
1 tablespoon ground cumin
½ teaspoon ground cinnamon
generous 1 cup long
grain rice
salt and ground black pepper
flat leaf parsley, to garnish

SERVES 6

1 Drain the lentils and put in a large pan. Add enough water to cover by 2 inches. Bring to a boil, cover the pan and simmer for 40 minutes to 1½ hours, or until tender. Drain thoroughly.

2 Finely chop one onion, and slice the other. Heat 1 tablespoon oil in a pan, add the chopped onion and fry until soft. Add the lentils, salt, pepper, cumin and cinnamon.

3 Measure the volume of rice and add it, with the same volume of water, to the lentil mixture. Cover and simmer for about 20 minutes, until both the rice and lentils are tender. Heat the remaining oil in a frying pan, and cook the sliced onion until very dark brown. Pour the rice mixture into a serving bowl, sprinkle with the onion and serve hot or cold, garnished with flat leaf parsley.

PILAF WITH SAFFRON AND PICKLED WALNUTS

*Pickled walnuts have a warm, tangy flavor that is lovely in rice and bulgur wheat dishes. This eastern
Mediterranean pilaf is interesting enough to serve on its own or with broiled lamb or pork.*

1 teaspoon saffron strands
½ cup pine nuts
3 tablespoons olive oil
1 large onion, chopped
3 garlic cloves, crushed
¼ teaspoon ground allspice
*1½-inch piece fresh ginger
root, grated*
generous 1 cup long grain rice
1¼ cups vegetable stock
*½ cup pickled walnuts, drained and
coarsely chopped*
¼ cup raisins
*3 tablespoons coarsely chopped parsley
or fresh cilantro*
salt and ground black pepper
parsley or cilantro, to garnish
plain yogurt, to serve

SERVES 4

1 Put the saffron in a bowl with 1 tablespoon boiling water and let stand. Heat a large frying pan and dry fry the pine nuts until they turn golden. Set them aside.

2 Heat the oil in the pan and fry the onion, garlic and allspice for 3 minutes. Stir in the ginger and rice and cook for 1 minute more.

3 Add the stock and bring to a boil. Reduce the heat, cover and simmer gently for 15 minutes until the rice is just tender.

4 Stir in the saffron and liquid, the pine nuts, pickled walnuts, raisins and parsley or cilantro. Season to taste with salt and pepper. Heat through gently for 2 minutes. Garnish with parsley or cilantro leaves and serve with plain yogurt.

VARIATION
Use one small eggplant, chopped and fried in a little olive oil, instead of the pickled walnuts, if you prefer.

OLIVE BREAD

Olive breads are popular all over the Mediterranean. For this Greek recipe use rich oily olives or those marinated in herbs rather than canned ones.

2 red onions, thinly sliced
2 tablespoons olive oil
1⅓ cups pitted black or green olives
7 cups strong flour
1½ teaspoons salt
4 teaspoons fast-rising dried yeast
3 tablespoons each coarsely chopped
parsley, coriander or mint

MAKES TWO 1½-POUND LOAVES

1 Fry the onions in the oil until soft. Coarsely chop the olives.

2 Put the flour, salt, yeast and parsley, coriander or mint in a large bowl with the olives and fried onions and pour in 2 cups hand-hot water.

VARIATION
Shape the dough into 16 small rolls. Slash the tops as above and reduce the cooking time to 25 minutes.

3 Mix to a dough using a round-bladed knife, adding a little more water if the mixture feels dry.

4 Turn out onto a lightly floured surface and knead for about 10 minutes. Put in a clean bowl, cover with plastic wrap and leave in a warm place until doubled in bulk.

5 Preheat the oven to 425°F. Lightly grease two baking sheets. Turn the dough onto a floured surface and cut in half. Shape into two loaves and place on the baking sheets. Cover loosely with lightly oiled plastic wrap and let rise until doubled in size.

6 Slash the tops of the loaves with a knife, then bake for about 40 minutes or until the loaves sound hollow when tapped on the bottom. Transfer to a wire rack to cool.

GREEK EASTER BREAD

In Greece, Easter celebrations are very important, and involve much preparation in the kitchen. This bread is sold in all the bakers' shops, and also made at home. It is traditionally decorated with red dyed eggs.

1 ounce fresh yeast

½ cup warm milk

6 cups strong flour

2 eggs, beaten

½ teaspoon caraway seeds

1 tablespoon sugar

1 tablespoon brandy

4 tablespoons butter, melted

1 egg white, beaten

2–3 hard-boiled eggs, dyed red

½ cup split almonds

MAKES 1 LOAF

1 Crumble the yeast into a bowl. Mix with one or two tablespoons of warm water, until softened. Add the milk and 1 cup of the flour and mix to a creamy consistency. Cover with a cloth, and let rest in a warm place to rise for 1 hour.

COOK'S TIP

You can often buy fresh yeast from health-food stores. It should be pale cream in color with a firm but crumbly texture.

2 Sift the remaining flour into a large bowl and make a well in the center. Pour the risen yeast into the well, and draw in a little of the flour from the sides. Add the eggs, caraway seeds, sugar and brandy. Incorporate the remaining flour, until the mixture begins to form a dough.

3 Mix in the melted butter. Turn on to a floured surface, and knead for about 10 minutes, until the dough becomes smooth. Return to the bowl, and cover with a cloth. Let rise in a warm place for 3 hours.

4 Preheat the oven to 350°F. Punch down the dough, turn onto a floured surface and knead for a minute or two. Divide the dough into three, and roll each piece into a long sausage. Make a braid as shown above, and place the loaf on a greased baking sheet.

5 Tuck the ends under, brush with the egg white and decorate with the eggs and split almonds. Bake for about 1 hour, until the loaf sounds hollow when tapped on the bottom. Cool on a wire rack.

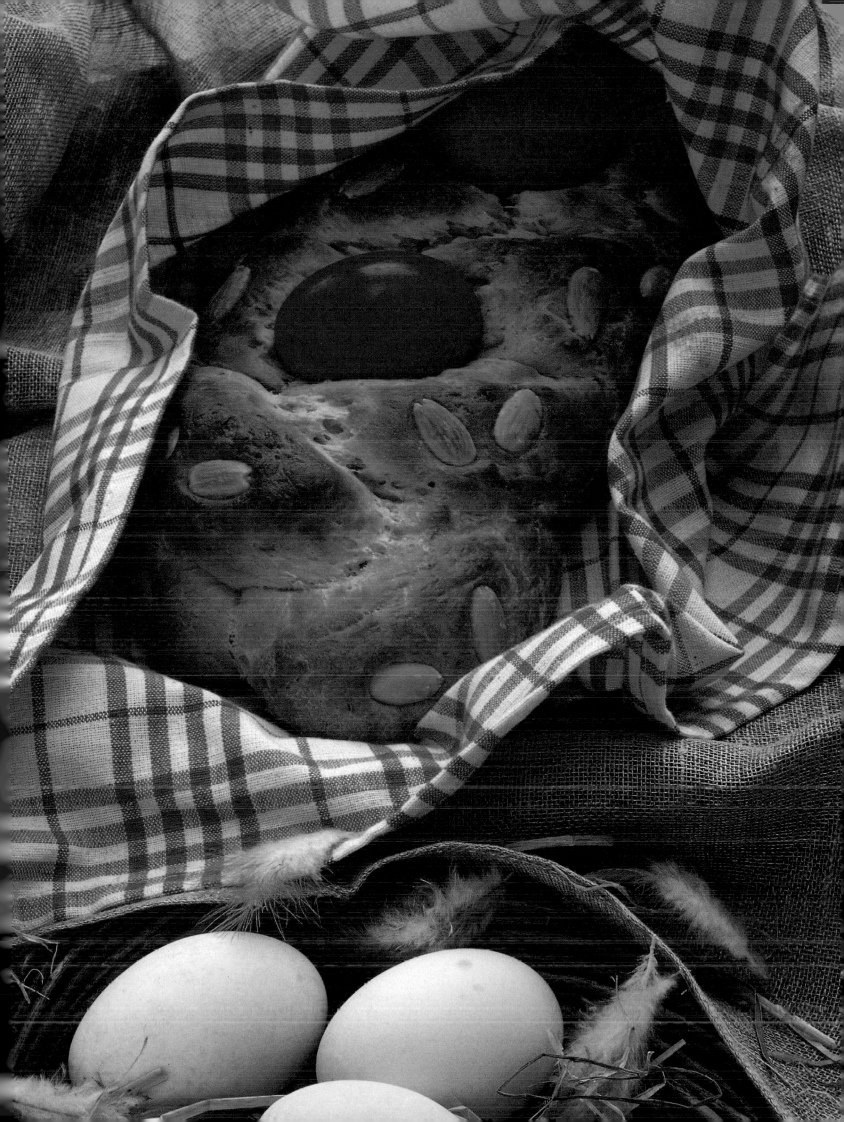

DESSERTS AND PASTRIES

*Desserts take full advantage of the
marvelous fresh fruit and nuts of Greece and
the Eastern Mediterranean, while honey, which is
also abundantly produced, is the preferred
sweetener, as in the recipes for Fresh Figs with
Honey and Wine, and Honey and Pine Nut
Tart. In Greece, Turkey, Lebanon and Egypt
small sweet pastries and sweetmeats are enjoyed as
a between-meal snack with good strong coffee.
Served in small pieces, they make a wonderful
contrast to the bitterness of the coffee. Semolina
and Nut Halva is a light version of a syrup-
steeped cake that is perfect either with coffee or as
a dessert with cream.*

FRESH FIGS WITH HONEY AND WINE

Any variety of figs can be used in this recipe, their ripeness determining the cooking time. Choose ones
that are plump and firm, and use quickly as they don't store well.

1⅞ cups dry white wine
⅓ cup honey
¼ cup sugar
1 small orange
8 whole cloves
1 pound fresh figs
1 cinnamon stick
mint sprigs, or bay leaves, to decorate

FOR THE CREAM
1¼ cups heavy cream
1 vanilla pod
1 teaspoon sugar

SERVES 6

1 Put the wine, honey and sugar in a heavy-based saucepan and heat gently until the sugar dissolves.

2 Stud the orange with the cloves and add to the syrup with the figs and cinnamon. Cover and simmer very gently for 5–10 minutes until the figs are softened. Transfer to a serving dish and allow to cool.

3 Put ⅔ cup of the cream in a small saucepan with the vanilla pod. Bring almost to a boil, then let cool and infuse for 30 minutes. Remove the vanilla pod and mix with the remaining cream and sugar in a bowl. Whip lightly. Transfer to a serving dish. Decorate the figs, then serve with the cream.

ROSE-FLAVORED ICE CREAM

Not strictly a traditional Middle Eastern recipe, but a delicious way of using Turkish delight.
Serve scattered with rose petals, if you have them.

4 egg yolks
½ cup sugar
1¼ cups milk
1¼ cups heavy cream
1 tablespoon rose water
6 ounces rose-flavored Turkish delight, chopped

SERVES 6

1 Beat the egg yolks and sugar until light. In a pan, bring the milk to a boil. Add to the egg and sugar, stirring, then return to the pan.

2 Continue stirring over low heat until the mixture coats the back of a spoon. Do not boil, or it will curdle. Allow to cool, then stir in the cream and rose water.

3 Put the Turkish delight in a pan with 2–3 tablespoons water. Heat gently, until almost completely melted, with just a few small lumps. Remove from the heat and stir into the cool custard mixture.

4 Let the mixture cool completely, then pour into a shallow freezer container. Freeze for 3 hours until just frozen all over. Spoon the mixture into a bowl.

5 Using a whisk, beat the mixture well, and return to the freezer container and freeze for 2 hours more. Repeat the beating process, then return to the freezer for about 3 hours, or until firm. Remove the ice cream from the freezer 20–25 minutes before serving. Serve with thin almond cookies or meringues.

HONEY AND PINE NUT TART

Honey of all kinds is produced throughout Greece and Turkey and provides the classic sweet taste of Eastern Mediterranean desserts.

FOR THE PASTRY
2 cups flour
½ cup butter
2 tablespoons confectioners' sugar
1 egg

FOR THE FILLING
1½ cup sweet butter, diced
½ cup sugar
3 eggs, beaten
*⅔ cup sunflower or other
flower honey*
grated rind and juice of 1 lemon
2⅔ cups pine nuts
pinch of salt
confectioners' sugar for dusting

SERVES 6

1   Preheat the oven to 350°F. Sift the flour into a bowl, add the butter and work with your fingertips until the mixture resembles fine bread crumbs. Stir in the confectioners' sugar. Add the egg and 1 tablespoon of water and work to a firm dough that leaves the bowl clean.

2   Roll out the pastry on a floured surface and use to line a 9-inch tart pan. Prick the base with a fork, and chill for 10 minutes. Line with foil or wax paper and fill with dried beans or rice, or baking beans if you have them. Bake the tart shell for 10 minutes.

3   Cream together the butter and sugar until light. Beat in the eggs one by one. Gently heat the honey in a small saucepan until runny, then add to the butter mixture with the lemon rind and juice. Stir in the pine nuts and salt, then pour the filling into the pastry shell.

4   Bake for about 45 minutes, until the filling is lightly browned and set. Allow to cool slightly in the pan, then dust generously with confectioners' sugar. Serve warm, or at room temperature, with sour cream or vanilla ice cream.

DATE AND ALMOND TART

Fresh dates make an unusual but delicious filling for a tart. The influences here are French and Middle Eastern — a true Mediterranean fusion!

FOR THE PASTRY
1½ cups flour
6 tablespoons butter
1 egg

FOR THE FILLING
scant ½ cup butter
7 tablespoons sugar
1 egg, beaten
scant 1 cup ground almonds
2 tablespoons flour
2 tablespoons orange-flower water
12–13 fresh dates, halved and pitted
4 tablespoons apricot jam

SERVES 6

1 Preheat the oven to 400°F. Place a baking sheet in the oven. Sift the flour into a bowl, add the butter and work with your fingertips until the mixture resembles fine bread crumbs. Add the egg and a tablespoon of cold water, then work to a smooth dough.

2 Roll out the pastry on a lightly floured surface and use to line an 8-inch tart pan. Prick the base with a fork, then chill until needed.

3 To make the filling, cream the butter and sugar until light, then beat in the egg. Stir in the ground almonds, flour and 1 tablespoon of the orange-flower water, mixing well.

4 Spread the mixture evenly over the base of the pastry shell. Arrange the dates, cut side down, on the almond mixture. Bake on the hot baking sheet for 10–15 minutes, then reduce the heat to 350°F. Bake for another 15–20 minutes until light golden and set.

5 Transfer the tart to a rack to cool. Gently heat the apricot jam, then strain. Add the remaining orange-flower water.

6 Brush the tart with the jam and serve at room temperature.

SEMOLINA AND NUT HALVA

Semolina is a popular ingredient in many desserts and pastries in the Eastern Mediterranean. Here it provides a spongy base for soaking up a deliciously fragrant spicy syrup.

FOR THE HALVA
½ cup sweet butter, softened
½ cup sugar
finely grated rind of 1 orange, plus
2 tablespoons juice
3 eggs
1 cup semolina
2 teaspoons baking powder
1 cup ground hazelnuts

TO FINISH
1½ cups sugar
2 cinnamon sticks, halved
juice of 1 lemon
4 tablespoons orange-flower water
½ cup unblanched hazelnuts,
toasted and chopped
½ cup blanched almonds, toasted
and chopped
shredded rind of 1 orange

SERVES 10

1. Preheat the oven to 425°F. Grease and line the base of a deep 9-inch square solid-based cake pan.

2. Lightly cream the butter in a bowl. Add the sugar, orange rind and juice, eggs, semolina, baking powder and hazelnuts and beat the ingredients together until smooth.

3. Put into the prepared pan and level the surface. Bake for 20–25 minutes until just firm and golden. Allow to cool in the pan.

4. To make the syrup, put the sugar in a small heavy-based saucepan with 2¼ cups water and the half cinnamon sticks. Heat gently, stirring, until the sugar has dissolved completely.

5. Bring to a boil and boil fast, without stirring, for 5 minutes. Measure half the boiling syrup and add the lemon juice and orange-flower water to it. Pour on the halva. Reserve the remainder of the syrup in the pan.

6. Leave the halva in the pan until the syrup is absorbed then turn it out onto a plate and cut diagonally into diamond-shape portions. Scatter with the nuts.

7. Boil the remaining syrup until slightly thickened then pour it on the halva. Scatter the shredded orange rind on the cake and serve with lightly whipped cream.

COOK'S TIP
Be sure to use a deep solid-based cake pan, rather than one with a loose base, otherwise the syrup might seep out.

Index